Create a
COASTLINE

By William Anthony

Minneapolis, Minnesota

Credits

All images are courtesy of Shutterstock.com unless otherwise specified. With thanks to Getty Images, Thinkstock Photo, and iStockphoto.

Cover – Pretty woman, Cinematographer, ohenze, Inspiring, VectorPlotnikoff, Nico Traut, Alena Nv. 4–5 – Maxim Babenko, Gaspar Janos. 6–7 – Claudia Pylinskaya, Alfmaler, Alexander Demyanenko, Atstock Productions, ian woolcock. 8–9 – Oscar Johns, EpicStockMedia, Nadzin. 10–11 – Photo Africa SA, Travel mania, MicroOne. 12–13 – Anastasia Boiko, shutterupeire, Ika Hilal, Wil Tilroe-Otte, matrioshka. 14–15 – Helen Hotson, Ken Schulze. 16–17 – Jovanovic Dejan, MaryDesy, Linda George, Lapa Smile. 18–19 – matsabe, Vaughan Sam, sixpixx, Pogorelova Olga. 20–21 – SunshineVector, NadyaEugene, liga_sveta, GoodStudio. 22–23 – olllikeballoon, Aluna1, owatta, Len.OK.

Library of Congress Cataloging-in-Publication Data is available at www.loc.gov or upon request from the publisher.

ISBN: 978-1-63691-482-4 (hardcover)
ISBN: 978-1-63691-487-9 (paperback)
ISBN: 978-1-63691-492-3 (ebook)

© 2022 Booklife Publishing
This edition is published by arrangement with Booklife Publishing.

North American adaptations © 2022 Bearport Publishing Company. All rights reserved. No part of this publication may be reproduced in whole or in part, stored in a retrieval system, or transmitted in any form or by any means, electronic, mechanical, photocopying, recording, or otherwise, without written permission from the publisher.

For more information, write to Bearport Publishing, 5357 Penn Avenue South, Minneapolis, MN 55419. Printed in the United States of America.

Contents

How to Build Our World 4
Build the Beach 6
Add the Ocean 8
Let the River Flow 10
Create the Cliff 12
Place the Plants 14
Invite the Animals 16
Start the Tourism 18
Protect the Place 20
Make Your Own Environment . . . 22
Glossary 24
Index 24

How to Build Our World

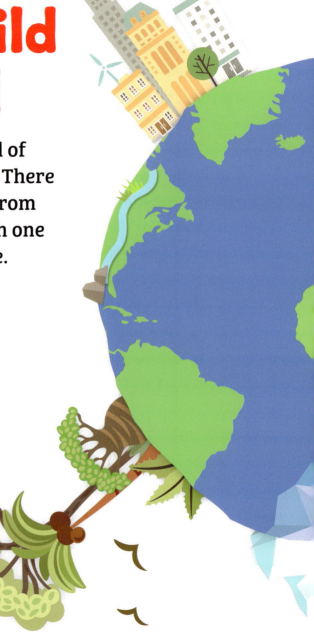

Our world is amazing. It is full of places to go and things to see. There are different **environments**, from rain forests to coastlines. Each one has plants, animals, and more.

What does a coastline environment look like? Let's build one to find out!

Build the Beach

Coastlines are places where the land meets the ocean. Let's build a beach for the land!

There are different kinds of beaches. Some beaches have lots of **pebbles**.

Some beaches are made of sand. The sand can be different colors, from golden yellow to black!

Beaches can also have large rocks.

Add the Ocean

Now that we've got some land, we need to add the ocean! The land and water will come together to create our coastline.

The ocean is big and full of salt water. Most of our world is covered with ocean.

During the day, the ocean moves farther in or out on the beach. When the water comes in, it is called high tide. When it goes out, it is called low tide.

When ocean waves flow onto the land, they move the sand and rocks there. This changes the shape of the coastline.

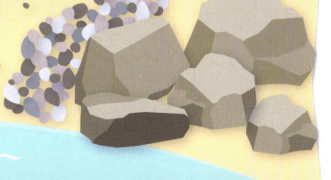

Let the River Flow

Our ocean looks great. But our coastline still has space for more water! Let's add a river that flows into the ocean.

Rivers start on land and end in an ocean or lake. The part of a river that flows into an ocean is called the mouth.

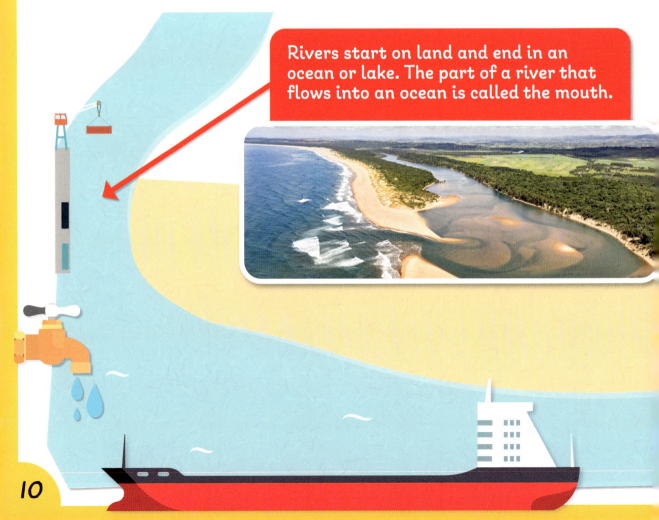

10

The water in rivers is usually not salty. It is fresh water.

Many river mouths have **ports**. Ships use ports to bring **supplies** to and from different places.

Create the Cliff

Not all coasts are flat, smooth beaches. Let's put a giant cliff on our coast!

Cliffs are the tall, rocky pieces of land along a coast.

Ocean waves can break rocks off cliffs. Rocks can also fall from the tops of cliffs.

Falling rocks can make cliffs dangerous! We must be very careful around them.

13

Place the Plants

Next, we'll add plants to our coastline. We may need different kinds of plants depending on whether our beach is rocky or sandy.

Moss often grows on coastline cliffs. Some trees and flowers may grow there, too.

Sand dunes are large piles of sand that form around tall grass. The grass stops sand from blowing away.

Grass also grows in wet areas near the ocean. These areas are called marshes.

Invite the Animals

The plants are in place. Now, let's add some animals to our coastline, too.

Jellyfish can get washed up on the beach when the tide goes out. These animals can sting you, so don't touch them!

Seagulls fly around coastlines. They may eat fish or other small ocean animals. They eat bugs, too.

Crabs live in little pools of water that are left in rocks when the tide goes out.

Start the Tourism

Our coastline looks awesome! We've made a great place for people to visit.

Coasts can have a lot of visiting **tourists**, especially during the hot summer.

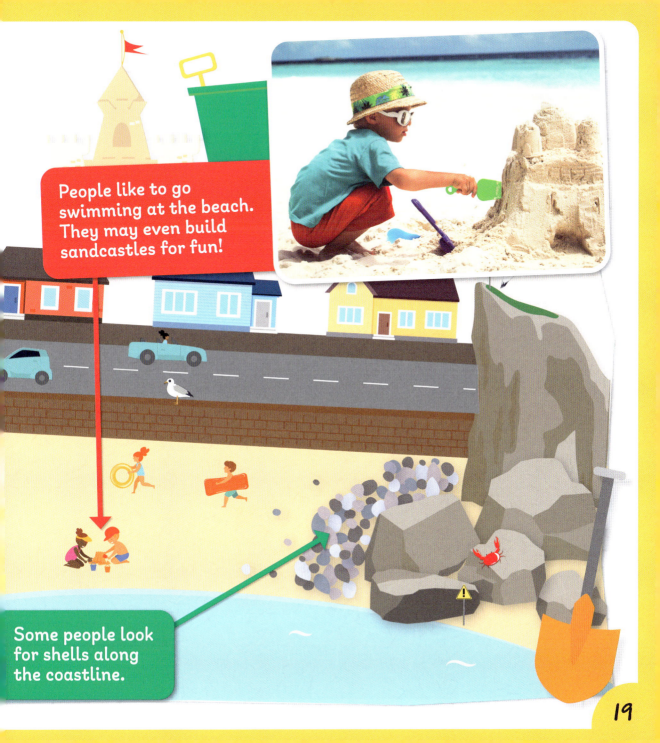

People like to go swimming at the beach. They may even build sandcastles for fun!

Some people look for shells along the coastline.

Protect the Place

During stormy weather, the ocean can **flood** areas near the coast where people are staying. Let's build something to protect these places.

A seawall is a tall wall along the coast. It blocks ocean waters from getting too close to buildings nearby.

Make Your Own Environment

Coastline environments are incredible! There are so many parts that make up the coastline. Now, it's time for you to build your own environment! You could draw it, paint it, or write about it. What do you want to put on your coastline?

Will your beach have pebbles, sand, or large rocks?

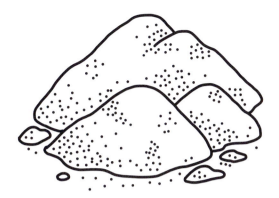

Will you add a giant cliff or a sand dune?

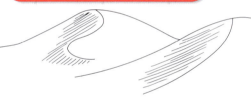

How will you protect the land from storms?

23

Glossary

concrete a hard material used in construction that is made from a mix of water and crushed rock

environments the different parts of our world in which people, animals, and plants live

flood to completely cover a usually dry area with a large amount of water

pebbles small, smooth rocks

ports places where ships load or unload things

supplies useful things, such as food or materials

tourists people who are visiting a place for vacation

Index

beaches 6–7, 9, 12, 14, 16, 19, 23
cliffs 12–14, 23
dunes 14, 23
fresh water 11
ports 11
rivers 10–11
salt water 8
sand 7, 14, 23
seawalls 20–21
storms 20–21, 23